Pricing a Project
How to prepare a professional quotation
Third edition

Melanie Thompson

First published in the UK in 2023 by
Chartered Institute of Editing and Proofreading
Studio 206, Milton Keynes Business Centre
Foxhunter Drive, Linford Wood
Milton Keynes
Buckinghamshire
MK14 6GD

ciep.uk

Copyright © 2023 Melanie Thompson

ISBN 978 1 838358 23 5 (print)
ISBN 978 1 838358 24 2 (PDF ebook)
ISBN 978 1 838358 25 9 (ePub)

Third edition

Second edition 2018, ISBN 978 0 993129 38 4 (print), 978 0 993129 39 1 (ebook)

First edition 2013, ISBN 978 0 993129 30 8; revisions 2016

All rights reserved. No part of this publication may be reproduced or used in any manner without written permission from the publisher, except for quoting brief passages in a review.

The moral rights of the author have been asserted.

The information in this work is accurate and current at the time of publication to the best of the author's and publisher's knowledge, but it has been written as a short summary or introduction only. Readers are advised to take further steps to ensure the correctness, sufficiency or completeness of this information for their own purposes.

Typeset in-house
Original design by Ave Design (avedesignstudio.com)
Image credits: Pexels and Shutterstock

Contents

Preface		1
1 |	Introduction	3
2 |	Taking a brief	5
	Understanding the client's requirements	8
3 |	Knowing your capabilities	11
	Keeping records	11
	Accounting for downtime	15
4 |	Knowing your limitations	17
5 |	Knowing the market and your competitors	19
	Basic rates	20
	Valuing your skills and knowledge	25
6 |	Preparing and submitting a quotation	26
	Pricing basics	26
	Contract basics	27
	Worked examples	28
	Additional considerations	35
	Estimating for project managers – points to note	39
	Participating in competitive tenders	40

7	What happens next?	42
	Negotiation basics	42
	Terms and conditions (T&Cs)	45
	And finally ...	45
8	Resources	46

Preface

It is ten years since the first edition of this guide was published, but in many ways that feels like a lifetime ago. The dramatic technological changes that began to impact the publishing industry in the 1980s appeared to have peaked by 2013 – with ubiquitous digital and online publishing, and social media invading all aspects of business processes. But the pace of change has not eased off: increasing business consolidation (meaning fewer 'traditional' publishers to work for) and globalisation have changed the marketplace for editorial professionals looking for (well-paid) work; while technological developments have had wide-ranging positive (and negative) impacts on working practices.

As I write, editorial colleagues are busily discussing how artificial intelligence (AI) is already influencing our daily work; while project teams dispersed across the globe gather via Teams or Zoom to discuss the forthcoming edition of a likely bestseller, or work interactively through Cloud-based platforms to tweak – in real time – the layout of an international organisation's annual report.

In this context, you might expect that guidance on working out the cost of your editorial services has also changed considerably. But it hasn't. True, there are many new ways to store business data and crunch numbers (for example, by using apps instead of spreadsheets or paper-based 'account books'), and some of the expenditure lines may have changed (far less business mileage to record, for instance). Yet the basic unit of editorial services – time – remains fixed.

The overarching approach to calculating the time you need to complete a number of tasks, as presented in this guide, has changed little. What has changed is the tasks themselves: for instance, when was the last time you worked on paper instead of onscreen?

This third edition includes updated worked examples of project pricing, based on more realistic 'rates' of payment and current client expectations, as well as updated and additional links to sources of information. The main thing that has not changed is the underlying message: value your time.

Happy quoting!

Melanie Thompson

June 2023

1 | Introduction

Receiving an enquiry from a client is possibly the most exciting thing that can happen to a new freelance editor or proofreader. (It can send an old-hand's heart aflutter, too!) Unfortunately, almost as soon as the client's phone call or email has been received, the excitement begins to wear off and panic sets in. Up goes the cry: What should I charge?

Unlike selling widgets at 'tuppence a bag', proofreading and copyediting are professional services and no two projects are the same. While it is perfectly sensible (correction: *essential*) for us 'service providers' to have a scale of fees based on the complexity of projects and the skills we are required to deploy, it can be difficult for new entrants to the industry to know how to tailor quotations to meet their clients' needs. Indeed, it is often the case that clients do not fully appreciate their own needs, and it is sometimes the duty of the professional service provider to advise the client on the extent of work required.

Pricing up a project involves four main elements:

- understanding what the particular job involves
- knowing your own pace of work
- knowing what can go wrong
- knowing the market rate for the work.

Taking these elements as its underlying structure, this CIEP guide describes the quotation process, from taking a brief to agreeing terms and conditions. Its advice is applicable to all types of editorial work – from simple proofreading, through copyediting and substantive editing of books, journals and other materials, to estimating the workload involved in website editing, and tendering for complex contracts. The guide also lists other sources of information and guidance.

This is a hands-on practical guide comprising tips, checklists and worked examples that will be of assistance not only to proofreaders, copyeditors and project managers working on any sort of publication from the 'conventional' publishing industry but also to clients in other spheres who seek the services of editorial professionals. With that in mind, it is important to clarify terminology before we go any further.

For well over 500 years the traditional publishing process employed a quality-control system that aimed to remove errors and inconsistencies at the earliest possible stage to reduce the cost of putting things right later on. In essence, the process starts with *text* in the form of a *manuscript* (handwritten, typed or generated onscreen) which is *copyedited* then given to a typesetter (or designer) who puts the text (and images) into a *layout* (book, magazine, web page, etc) to create a 'proof'. *Proofreading*, traditionally, is the final check that the other professionals in the process have done their job correctly and that as many errors as possible have thereby been eliminated.

The advent of computerised text generation – and, by the mid-1980s, desktop publishing – opened up the publishing process to everyone with access to the right technology. Indeed, anyone with a smartphone can now publish material to the whole wide world (whether they *should* do so is an entirely different issue).

Although it is now possible to publish material almost instantaneously, clients continue to recognise the need for quality control and seek the assistance of editorial professionals. Many clients may not recognise the job titles of copyeditor, desk editor, subeditor, typesetter, proofreader and so on, but the tasks these roles traditionally performed still exist, whether the client is following the step-by-step 'traditional' publishing process or a last-minute quality-control check. This blurring of boundaries makes the task of pricing a project more difficult than it used to be – is it a copyedit, a line edit, a proofread, a 'proof-edit' or even a rewrite? Only you and your client will know the answer! For that reason, this guide uses the traditional terms 'copyediting' and 'proofreading' in the full knowledge that their meanings are open to interpretation.

2 | Taking a brief

Whether the enquiry arrives via an email, a tweet, a phone call, while you're standing at the school gate, or in a bar/bus queue (choose your networking opportunity of preference), it is very tempting to bat back a rapid response of 'Ah, I can do that for £xx'.

But that approach is wrong in so many ways, not least because it doesn't look or sound very professional. Even if you are happy to state your rate (and for reasons why this might not be a good idea, see chapter 6 and chapter 7), a quick-fire response could land you in a tricky spot later on if it turns out that the work is more complex and/or time-consuming than your knee-jerk assumptions. Equally, you may not have fully accounted for the needs – and budget – of the client and may therefore not win the job, in spite of your prompt reply.

An enquiry is the opening of a conversation between two parties: the buyer and the seller. As many sales manuals will tell you, it is in the seller's interest to engage the buyer in a conversation in order to both win their confidence and 'close the deal'. If that all sounds a bit too much like *The Apprentice*, fear not: it's not all about the bottom line.

The objective of a professional service provider is to understand the client's needs and deliver a service that is specifically tailored to meet these needs. Clients generally appreciate a supplier who takes time to understand their needs and circumstances, even if they eventually have to make their decision on the basis of cost rather than on less-tangible factors.

As well as being a chance to investigate the client's requirements, this opening conversation is also an opportunity for you to shine – as a confident professional and as a human being who will be a competent, reliable and friendly member of their 'team', however short-lived the project may be. It may also be a good time to 'upsell' yourself or your services: for instance, if the client thinks they need proofreading, but your editor's antennae suggest that copyediting would be more appropriate.

Although two projects are rarely alike, that does not mean you should have a totally different approach to each new enquiry. It will be far more efficient (in terms of your own time) to adopt a structured approach to dealing with enquiries. This can be invaluable for your ongoing marketing efforts.

One successful approach is to generate an enquiry form built around a list of prompts to help you keep the conversation on track. The form can be filed alongside the quotation you generate, may accompany the job as it progresses through various stages and may prove essential if there were ever (heaven forfend) a dispute with the client about the scope/extent of the service you had agreed upon.

Whether you opt for a formal form-filling approach or merely take notes of incoming enquiries, the sort of information you need in order to produce a sensible quotation remains broadly the same. **Figure 1** shows a model enquiry form,* but other formats or systems work just as well. This model form answers the standard questions: who, what, when, where and how? It also reminds you that it might be necessary to ask 'why?' and to obtain a few other pertinent details (as discussed in **'Understanding the client's requirements'** below).

---

*On figures 1 and 2, italic text inside [ ] represents hints/guidance for how to fill out the form.

2 | Taking a brief

Figure 1. Model enquiry form

	Enq. date:	Enq. no:
Client/company name:		
Contact name:		
Phone no:		
Email:		
Website (URL):		
Postal address:	[*Fill in later*]	
Source:		
Project title:		
Description:	[*eg proofread, copyedit, project management?*] [*topic, audience, etc*] [*one-off/series?*]	
Length:	[*Words/pages*]	
Artwork:	[*Yes/No? Details, permissions?*]	
Work IN as:	[*Hard copy, email, secure server*]	
Work OUT as:	[*Word (tracked), PDF, etc*]	
Client to supply:	[*Style sheet, author's contact details, etc*]	
Schedule:		
Contract:	[*Client's/freelancer (eg CIEP model); simple*]	
Payment terms:	[*Standard/discount/out-of-hours premium*]	
Sample provided:	[*Yes/No; date*]	
Estimate/quote:	[*Value*]	
Accepted:	[*Date*]	**Job sheet no:**

Bear in mind that the order of questions is not fixed. If you are lucky enough to be busy already, you may need to focus on the client's deadline; if the subject matter is not your main area of expertise, you may need to clarify that early on (see **chapter 4**).

A word of warning: despite the various merits of the conversational approach, it is crucial to keep the chat appropriate and succinct, especially if you do not know the client. You may not have spoken to a soul apart from your local parcel courier for several days, but clients are invariably busy people and may well have several suppliers to contact in a row.

Understanding the client's requirements

Some projects are clear and straightforward; others are less so. Nevertheless, in order to be sure of what is required, it is worth double-checking the client's requirements using the prompts in **figure 1**.

For more complex projects, and for clients who may need additional support or guidance as to the publishing process and your role within that, a few additional questions may be needed.

Scope/scale of the editing/proofreading required?

This question is crucial because it can have a considerable impact on project timings and costs. The client may not have read the material in detail, so will not necessarily be aware of the level of editing required. Some clients, though, may specify 'essential spelling, grammar and house style only' or 'a light proofread only'. Even if the client has been specific about the level of editing/proofreading, you may need to advise that additional work should be carried out.

How will queries be handled?

The client may have a preferred way of handling queries, or they may need you to suggest a way forward. Either way will have an impact on the time needed to complete the work. For instance, if you will not have direct contact with the author, it may take longer to draft a list of queries (because any intermediary may not be intimately acquainted with the material).

Who else might you need to liaise with?

Are there several authors, in-house/external project managers, designers, illustrators, typesetters …? The more people involved, the more time the project will take and the greater the potential for process iterations. Don't forget to check on the availability of people in the chain (for example, X works only Tuesday–Thursday; the lead author is off on sabbatical for three months from …).

Is there a specific event associated with the output?

Students are notorious for last-minute calls to freelance proofreaders, suggesting a turnaround time of hours rather than days for 'proofreading' that is really copyediting. But publisher clients and other organisations can also omit such critical details from their briefs. For example, is the client racing to get a book out ahead of a competitor? The importance of hitting a deadline may be something you wish to factor into your costings/quotation, so it is well worth asking how 'fixed' is a fixed deadline (see an example in '**Estimating for non-standard projects**').

There are many more questions you might need to ask: suffice to say that over time you will build up a feeling for potential pitfalls and unexpected complexities. The crucial thing is to ask as many questions up front as possible, in order to grasp the 'known unknowns', without leaving too many 'unknown unknowns' lurking to bite you.

Tips

- Always answer the call/reply to an email as soon as you can. Don't let the enquiry lurk on your voicemail or in your inbox. If you are busily trying to meet a deadline, don't be afraid to say: 'I'm just finishing an urgent project; please can I return your call/email this afternoon?' Clients are generally happy if you briefly explain your circumstances and give them a fixed time/day when you can respond or begin the discussion.
- The first enquiry is speed-dating without the visuals: keep it short, sweet and to the point, and don't forget that first impressions count. Bear in mind that the first approach from a client may be the beginning of a long and fruitful relationship, even if you are not free or able to take on the first job they ask about.
- It is always a good idea, if possible, to see a sample of the material before you quote. If you get the opportunity, ask for something from the middle of the text (authors often spend longer polishing the beginning/end).
- What goes around, comes around: do offer to help find someone else, if appropriate (see **chapter 4**).
- The time spent dealing with enquiries is never wasted. If you have a gap in your schedule, find old enquiry forms and get in touch with a few that 'got away', to see whether there is any possibility of work.

3 | Knowing your capabilities

'Time is money' is an ancient cliché, but time *is* the main commodity of the freelance proofreader/editor's business. How much clients are willing or able to pay for that time depends on the general availability of 'time' in the marketplace (the more freelancers with free time, the lower the unit price) but also on the freelancer-specific factors: editorial skills plus proven experience and, where appropriate, subject-specific knowledge. Thus, even within the relatively small CIEP network, there are gradations of pay expectations – from new entrants to the industry whose fees may be largely time-based, to experienced practitioners who may be in higher demand (so have less time available) coupled with lots of proven experience, knowledge and specialisms.

This is good from the clients' point of view, because it enables them to choose a service provider who meets their needs in terms of time (cost) and skills/ knowledge. For freelancers at the start of their careers, this can be frustrating because remuneration may be lower to begin with; but for seasoned professionals, the annual accumulation of experience and skills ('working smarter') may be the only way to increase 'profits'. After all, there are only so many hours in a day: simply 'working harder' may not be an option.

If time, then, is the primary factor in any quotation, it is crucial for all service providers to have a good understanding of (a) the time needed to achieve various editorial tasks and (b) the unavoidable downtime of running a professional editorial business.

Keeping records

How long should it take to proofread an eight-page PDF onscreen? How much time should I allow to copyedit a 120,000-word manuscript written by a scientific expert who uses English as an additional language?

It is not surprising that such questions are 'frequent fliers' in professional forums and social media. New entrants to the industry often find it very difficult to gauge whether they are working too slowly (or too quickly). The question is no easier for experienced professionals to answer.

Sure, there are tools that can help you to work more quickly by semi-automating repetitive tasks, but they will never eliminate the painstaking and time-consuming word-by-word work that forms the bulk of any proofreading or editing project. As we are already learning, even the most cutting-edge artificial intelligence (AI) tools make mistakes (or even make

> ### A few words about reading
>
> Despite the claims of speed-reading gurus, there are physical limits on the capacity of humans to read text accurately.
>
> Reading speed is limited by the ability of the human eye to move along a line of text and focus on each element directly in front of it (it needs to do this for around 250 milliseconds), as well as by the inner workings of the brain that translate the incoming visual data into meaningful content.
>
> In normal circumstances – that is, when presented with words in a standard format such as the page of a book or a website – university-educated adults who are considered to be good readers 'usually move along at about 200 to 400 words per minute'.
>
> Editorial work, however, is not 'normal' reading, and will usually be at the slower end of typical human reading speed. In addition, editorial workers do not just take in text: they act upon it in various ways, and also spend time thinking about the possible options for changing it, or looking in reference resources to check usage and style preferences.
>
> It's easy to see how those seconds and minutes pile up. And the longer (or more complex) the text, the slower the focused reading may be.
>
> *(Source: Rayner K, Schotter ER and Treiman R (2016) 'So much to read, so little time: How do we read, and can speed reading help?' Psychological Science in the Public Interest, vol. 17, issue 1. https://doi.org/10.1177/1529100615623267)*

things up), so there is – at the time of writing – no viable substitute for the considerable input of a human brain with all its non-mechanical foibles.

In order to produce a sensible – and acceptable – quotation for a potential client, it is crucial to have an insight into how long the job will take *you*. Note the emphasis there: just as each project is different, so each proofreader/editor's approach will be different. There is no magic formula that can be applied to calculate 'universal editing time'. And remember that you need to take into account screen breaks, time to make and consume refreshments and comfort breaks, on top of running-a-business time.

'Aha!' you may say. 'But the client says this job will take 20 hours'. Some clients do approach the enquiry/quotation process with an opening gambit such as this, but as professional service providers, we need to be clear in our own minds that their estimate is appropriate to the circumstances of the project in question. After all, how can the client know that it will take *you* 20 hours? Do they actually know for a fact that similar jobs have taken other freelancers 20 hours? It is possible that others spent more or less time, but *billed for 20 hours*. This is not to suggest that people are being dishonest in either their estimates or their bills, but rather that the time × rate equation is not quite as straightforward as it may appear.

For instance, Freelancer A may assess a project as needing 30 hours and charge £35 per hour, while Freelancer B works a little more slowly, estimating 35 hours, but at a rate of £30 per hour. If both were to submit a quote for £1,050 with no further explanation, the client might choose either A or B. But if the candidates explain how they arrived at their cost estimate, the client may decide on either one of them, depending on the circumstances (for example, choose A if turnaround time is critical, or choose B if the client has corporate guidelines on what it considers an acceptable 'rate').

There is an ongoing debate among freelancers (of all professions) regarding hourly rate vs fixed fee (see '**Worked examples**'), but for now let's concentrate on the time factor.

There are numerous free or low-cost timing apps. There are also various pre-formatted templates in Excel or other business management software packages, including a toolkit developed by CIEP (see **Resources and further reading** for links to some of these resources). But it is also possible to keep good and detailed records using old-fashioned analogue technology (pen and paper). **Figure 2** presents a possible paper-based project timesheet, as an illustration of how this sort of tool can be used.

Note that the pro forma relates to just one project. In this system a separate sheet is needed for each additional project. This enables you to track predicted performance (from your quotation) against the actual performance.

The system is particularly beneficial in that it allows you to be very specific about what tasks are being achieved. It is therefore an invaluable resource to help you answer 'how long will it take to …?' questions, but also provides a detailed record of what was done when – serving both as a checklist of tasks completed and as a permanent record in case there are subsequent client queries about whether something was addressed, or why was there a delay on project Z.

Tips

- New to editing/proofreading? Take every opportunity to begin gathering data about your performance. Use 'real' projects wherever possible. For example, time yourself doing a client's test, or complete a 'dummy' timesheet when assessing a potential project. Do not rely on your usual novel-reading speed, even for general assessments (as mentioned above 'professional' reading is invariably slower, for very good reasons!).
- Very experienced? Use your timesheets as part of an annual 'performance audit'. Could you have done things differently on project X? Would training or a software upgrade help you to work more quickly/consistently?
- Problem project? Having a running total of time spent will very quickly flag a potential overrun so that you can take swift action (see **chapter 7**).

Figure 2. Model project timesheet

			Enq. no.		Project no. 1
Client/project title:					
Schedule (key dates):			[*Item: eg text received; PDF returned*]		[*Date*]
Date	Start/end	Hrs	Running total	Notes [*tasks completed, for example … *]	
20/3	9–10	1	1	Familiarisation with client's style sheet	
	10.15–12.15	2	3	1st read-through/assessment of MS; 0–6,000 words	
	1.30–2.45	1.25	4.25	ditto – 6,000–12,000 words	
	3–3.30	0.5	4.75	Run client's clean-up macro / other prep for editing	
21/3	9.30–12.30	3	7.75	Onscreen editing (up to 4,000 words) etc	
				[*add more lines if necessary*]	

Notes
- Depending on your numbering preferences, the project number may or may not match the enquiry number. (Unless you are extremely lucky, not all enquiries will result in a project.)
- Decide the level of detail that works for you (hourly, half-hourly, to nearest five minutes). Note that there are gaps in this timesheet, which may have been time spent answering the phone, making tea, working on something different.

Accounting for downtime

Office hours may be 9am to 5pm, but it is highly unlikely that employee (in-house) editors or proofreaders would have focused on the job for a solid eight hours a day. Apart from anything else, this would be a health risk! At the very least they will take lunch and comfort breaks. The same goes for freelancers, and all the more so because freelancers may have several projects on the go, plus other business-related tasks to be dealt with.

It is therefore a very good habit to keep a separate timesheet to account for daily non-project activities. Sometimes it may even be a good idea to make a 'project' for yourself, right down to the costing, planning and implementation. For instance, new freelancers might try that approach for their first marketing campaign. It can be a useful discipline to help control your own time and any related spending.

Non-project time might involve:

- responding to enquiries (sales leads)
- generating enquiries (marketing/networking/business development)
- formal training (continuing professional development, CPD)
- informal training (self-study, participating in professional networks such as CIEP forums)
- business admin (monthly invoices/annual accounts; researching/buying new office equipment).

Having a sensible estimate of non-project time means that, if you have a gap in your schedule, you can usefully fill it with items from your queue of non-project tasks. It also helps you to know what can be safely dropped, if a dream job comes along.

The question of whether and how to account for non-project time in your fee is discussed in '**Worked examples**'.

4 | Knowing your limitations

Here's another (true) cliché: honesty is the best policy.

A client may be desperate for someone – anyone – to proofread an urgent document, but if you are fully committed already, or if the material is unfamiliar to you, the professional approach is to say 'no, thank you'. For added professional kudos, you could offer to try to find someone to take on the project (*with the client's permission*) by recommending trusted colleagues or finding a good match through the CIEP's marketplace or IM Available list (a free listing for CIEP Intermediate Members, made available to CIEP Professional and Advanced Professional Members). You could mention the project on other networks such as LinkedIn, or simply point the client towards the CIEP Directory.

If you have successfully extracted the core information from the client during your initial conversation/email exchange (see **chapter 2**), you may be in a position to say 'no, thank you' immediately. Common reasons for this decision include:

- You can't possibly meet the schedule (and nor could anyone else!).
- You are too busy (not the same as the previous reason).
- The material is too far outside your comfort zone (though don't automatically turn down a 'challenge' that might be an excellent CPD opportunity, *if both you and the client understand there may be additional effort (time) required*).
- The project requires skills/equipment you don't have and are not interested in obtaining.

Tactically, there are two other questions to ask yourself regarding saying 'no, thank you':

- When? Answer: as soon as possible.
- How? Answer: quickly, politely and professionally.

Easy, isn't it? But a surprising number of freelancers fire off quotations or respond to general enquiries without really thinking through the implications of winning the job. Such an approach would be (a) a waste of your own time (spent preparing a quotation for a job you don't really want or are not really qualified for) and (b) a waste of the client's time, especially if they have only contacted one or two freelancers who then dawdle over their responses only to say 'no, thank you' a few days later.

> **Tip**
> - Don't be tempted to overprice a job that you do not really want, on the off-chance that you might win it anyway. That way potential disaster lies, especially if you have to let down other good regular clients to meet the needs of this one stressful high payer. Your reputation as a professional is at stake (particularly since the advent of social networking), as is your health. Over-committing yourself, or taking on a job you dread, is a sure-fire way to pile on the stress.

By all means explain to the client the reason for your decision not to quote – politely and concisely. For instance, let them know if the schedule is too tight to complete the tasks required, or if other skills (such as indexing or page layout) may be more appropriate. This can be beneficial to the client, because the information may influence their approach to other freelancers and/or subsequent projects. Providing this bit of free 'consultancy' will enhance your professional reputation (provided, of course, your suggestions are appropriate).

But if you decide you are interested in the project and that you have the skills and technology to take it on, you can finally move forward to preparing the quotation!

5 | Knowing the market and your competitors

Whether you decide to calculate your charges per hour, per page or per project is a decision for you and your clients. There are pitfalls to each approach, and benefits too (as discussed in chapter 6 and chapter 7). But the most difficult decision, especially for new freelancers, is what rate to seek. It is a controversial topic, often discussed in editorial forums and blog posts. The difficulty arises because, to some extent, we are reluctant to share salary-related information. Why this is so is a complex question – touching on both cultural factors and legal requirements – that is beyond the scope of this short guide.

Suffice to say that many other freelance professionals (from mobile hairdressers to accountants and building surveyors) develop a reasonable understanding of the 'going rate' for the service they provide by gathering 'market intelligence' from a variety of sources (of which more below). Beyond that, professionals discount or increase the rate depending on a range of factors such as availability of supply, geographical location, speciality of the service offered and so on.

> It is never reasonable – nor is it sensible – to make assumptions about a client's budget.
>
> Kia Thomas, CIEP Advanced Professional Member, 2023

For freelance editors, proofreaders and project managers there is no easy answer to the question of 'what is the going rate?'. It will depend on the nature of the project and the client, but there are some general guidelines that can help you work out what to charge.

Basic rates

On the face of it, the easiest way to decide what to charge is to find out what other people are charging for similar work. But pause a moment and re-read that previous sentence: 'find out what other people are charging'. Then what? Charge the same? Undercut them? Or are you worth much more?

In a buyers' market where there is a lot of competition there is the risk of a race to the bottom. (Some may say that's exactly what the 'gig economy' may do, but let's not get bogged down with economics and politics at this stage!) And is aiming for the same rate as unknown others a good indication of the value *you* are adding to your clients' projects? Setting a rate is as much about valuing yourself (your skills and expertise) as covering your costs and scraping a living.

Here are two ways to begin thinking about the rate-setting process: the bottom-up approach and the comparators approach. Think of the bottom-up approach as the basic economics of being a business (what is the 'cost price' of an hour of your time), whereas the comparators approach is akin to using price comparison websites. A successful pricing strategy requires a bit of each, with a sprinkle of 'value added' on top.

Bottom-up approach

It is unlikely that editorial professionals will ever be in the Premiership footballer salary bracket but, given the education, training and skills we deploy and – crucially – *the value we add* to clients' projects, it is fair to say that our work is worth more than the National Living Wage (NLW), which was introduced in April 2016 and is legally enforceable for employers (although it does not apply in the same way to 'clients'). Despite the government's commitment to increase the NLW every year, commentators acknowledge that it remains inadequate for many people (that is, it is not enough to keep above the poverty threshold without the need for state benefits).

The Centre for Research in Social Policy promotes a Minimum Income Standard (MIS), based on research first carried out by the Joseph Rowntree Foundation (JRF), which originally championed the living wage. The MIS budgets for different household types are reviewed every year.

5 | Knowing the market and your competitors

In the second edition of this CIEP guide, we quoted the JRF study of 2017, which concluded that single people needed to earn at least £17,900 a year before tax to achieve MIS, and couples with two children at least £20,400 each (so £40,800 in total). The most recent study, published in September 2022 using data up to April 2022,* used a different calculation method. It attempted to account for the ongoing impacts of the Covid-19 pandemic and cited the comparable incomes of £25,500 for a single person – *an increase of 43%* – and £43,400 (up by about 4%) for a couple with two children. Predictions of volatility in the global economy strongly suggest that future JRF studies could reveal similar sharp increases, particularly in the mid-2020s.

Needless to say (but say it I shall), wages have not kept pace with the cost of living.

It is important to note that these national figures are usually applied for low-skilled or unskilled work, but it is also crucial to appreciate that they are for *wages* – paid to an employee by an employer. That's a very important difference, which is not always fully appreciated by clients who are busily concentrating on their own bottom lines.

As a freelancer you are, in effect, both employee and employer – your business 'employs' you. So, in addition to thinking about the hourly rate you need to earn, you also have to factor in the assorted business costs that are opaque to directly employed staff. Typically, these will include:

- National Insurance
- pension provision
- training/CPD
- office costs (utilities such as electricity, telephone and internet services, hardware and software, stationery, etc)
- professional indemnity insurance (if applicable).

In addition, freelance service providers have to delve into the 'profits' from their business if they are to benefit from holiday pay, sick pay and

---

* The report was published in September 2022 but refers to data up to April 2022. The difference is important, because there was considerable instability in the financial markets and cost of living from August to October 2022.

maternity/paternity or bereavement leave. And the above list does not even begin to take account of other non-pay benefits that employers might offer (such as travel season ticket subsidies, childcare vouchers, healthcare assistance, share options …). Avoiding these direct costs is one of the main advantages to clients of using freelance service providers, and that's before we even begin to factor in the flexibility and added value of using specialist freelance workers.

But that's not all! You cannot directly equate the hourly rate with annual income. Few people are fully productive for 52 weeks of the year. (Note: there are 252 days in a typical UK working year.) A rule of thumb often applied is that office workers are productive for three-fifths of their total paid hours, with the other two-fifths of the time going on management-related meetings, minor admin tasks, travelling between buildings/departments/customers and the all-important watercooler moments. For freelance editorial professionals, there are some productivity gains (no more annual performance meetings to endure, for instance) but the freelancer's productivity rate is eroded due to 'waiting time' between projects; and the non-project-related factors mentioned in '**Accounting for downtime**' also need to be accounted for on top of all that.

The bottom-up approach can be used to set your break-even point or the 'absolute rock bottom' rate (which might be a useful guideline for new freelancers) but it lacks the market-driven 'going rate' factor.

Comparators approach

If you hang out in freelance internet forums or follow freelance bloggers, you will often hear whispers about the perfect 'suggested rates' – where groups of freelancers or businesses have pooled their knowledge and calculated what they consider to be a fair hourly pay. Sounds useful doesn't it? Such 'suggestions' do exist, and they are helpful, but not without controversy. In fact, many professional bodies produce some sort of pricing data for their members, but they inevitably have to adopt a one-size-fits-all approach by suggesting rates aligned with broad-brush tasks. If they are based on data collected from members, they are only reviewing a small sector of the wider market (so they tend to exclude what non-members may charge). They also lag behind changes in the economy.

5 | Knowing the market and your competitors

It is far better to combine actual market data, whether from directly equivalent or from approximately similar job roles, and then factor in your specific business costs and expertise as appropriate.

Two rules of thumb are often mentioned in this context:

- Take the equivalent employee hourly rate and double it (the idea being that the doubling mops up the employer-related costs, so an office worker paid £18 per hour equates to a freelancer rate of £36 per hour).
- Take the equivalent annual employee's salary and divide by 1,000 (for example, a £40,000 staff salary equates to a freelancer rate of £40 per hour).

The first method is a reasonable guideline and such rates will still be tempting to employers compared with taking on additional (temporary) employees because there are still savings to be made in terms of productivity, ease of recruitment and swift access to expertise. The second method, however, is less reliable for industry sectors such as publishing, where staff salaries have always been below average.

A more detailed approach was put forward by the writer and journalist Andrew Bibby. For several years he published information that cleverly combined the typical overheads paid by many editorial and journalist freelancers with the typical salaries paid across the industry to create his Freelance Ready Reckoner (see **Resources and further reading** for a link). That resource was last updated in 2020, but it remains a useful starting point for knowing your worth and the notes provided are extremely useful when trying to understand the true cost of operating as a freelance professional in publishing and related fields.

But there is no real substitute for researching your particular market sector to get an idea of the rates for similar or comparable work. For example, always read incoming recruitment emails from CIEP (and comparable organisations), even if you are not seeking an in-house role. Adverts may state the salary range, and training and experience needed, plus a range of employee benefits such as enhanced pension contributions and flexible home/office working.) Likewise, keep an eye out for reports of industry salaries and 'rate for the job' surveys (some suggestions are in **Resources and further reading**; read the situations vacant advertisements posted on LinkedIn or recruitment websites (not just for similar jobs but for those of a similar level of skill or expertise); talk to recruitment agents; and don't forget to learn as much as you can from your fellow freelancers. Bidding for work as a group can be an eye-opener, for instance, because you will have to talk openly with each other about what rate you are willing to accept or aim to achieve.

Tailor your research to fit the sort of work you are interested in. For example, if you want to work for local businesses, find out what other local service providers (graphic designers or website companies) charge; if you are targeting self-publishers or students, think what other professional services they might be familiar with (private tuition, for instance) and align your rates with that; and if you work for international law firms or government bodies, take account of the likely bills submitted to your client by sub-contractors in other professions (billing too cheaply can undermine your credibility).

Valuing your skills and knowledge

It is helpful to have a range of rates based on either client type or project type, underpinned by a break-even rate. That makes it easy to work out, on a project-by-project or client-by-client basis, precisely what rate should be applied to a quotation. Determining factors include:

- complexity of the project
- level of skill/experience required
- financial status of the client (eg small local charity vs multinational corporation)
- urgency of the job (might you apply a premium for evening/weekend/ Bank Holiday working?).

Such factors may also be useful bargaining points during subsequent negotiations with the client (see '**Negotiation basics**').

It is important to note that, just as in-house career paths relate mainly to gaining experience and responsibility, so it is with any freelance business: expending effort on training, gaining expertise in a subject/piece of software and so on should command a premium (not unlike employees receiving an element of performance-related pay for achieving annual goals).

Reassess your own 'going rates' frequently (at least annually), not just to test the market but to reflect any additional training you have undertaken and the experience gained on live projects over the preceding period.

6 | Preparing and submitting a quotation

Having read the previous chapters, it should now be clear why giving a potential client a quote spontaneously or advertising set rates on your website may not be a good idea: there is much more to pricing a job than the 'rate'. Even more important, having stated a price it can be very difficult (though not impossible) to revise it in any way other than down (see '**Worked examples**' and '**Negotiation basics**').

However, there are ways that a professionally prepared quotation can help prevent the need for re-evaluation while the project is in progress, as we will see.

Pricing basics

The basic equation for pricing most editorial projects is:

> time × rate + expenses

To cost a specific project, modify the equation by breaking down the time into different tasks (which *may* merit different rates) and applying various factors to the basic rate (to account for level of editorial skill/proven experience, subject-specific or format-specific premium, client's known budget, etc). For more complex projects, there may then be an allowance for 'contingency' (see '**Complex estimating**' and '**Negotiation basics**').

Thus, even a quotation that states a fixed fee or a 'guideline cost' may actually include:

> time × rate 1
> time × rate 2
> contingency (= time × rate 2)
> expenses

Contract basics

Having calculated the costs, you need to inform the client. It is important to note that, legally, an offer (your quoted fee) plus an agreement constitute a contract – *even a verbal/handshake agreement*. Of course, it is much better to have your offer and the client's agreement on paper or as an exchange of emails. The contract can be as simple as:

> **Service provider:** *I will do this job for £x by next Thursday.*
> **Client:** *OK, that's great. Please go ahead.*

An exchange of emails along those lines may be fine for smaller projects, or where you already have an ongoing relationship with the client. However, such an agreement is open to (mis)interpretation and dispute. It is therefore good practice to ensure that both parties to the contract understand what has been agreed, particularly for complex projects (even if you know the client well) or if the client has never commissioned editorial services before.

A formal document may not be necessary (though organisations such as the CIEP do provide contract templates); it is the information that you exchange with the client which is key. Ideally, a professional contract will:

- set out what the client has asked you to do
- describe any additional work that you suggest should be carried out (if appropriate)
- state the schedule, key delivery dates or deliverables
- state your terms and conditions (T&Cs) or refer to the fact that you agree to/have signed the client's T&Cs
- state the time + rate (or fixed fee)
- state what you will charge for any anticipated expenses (eg train fare to attend a meeting), if applicable
- add an amount for contingency if appropriate (see '**Complex estimating**').

Breaking down the costs in this way not only provides you with a framework upon which to organise the work; it also sets up the detail of what you will/won't do and are/are not charging for, in the event of a dispute.

The other advantage of this approach is that each point may be negotiated separately before the two parties (you and the client) make an agreement (see '**Negotiation basics**').

Worked examples
Simple estimating – page rates and fixed fees

Freelancer A has an academic background in psychology at postgraduate level, and she has recently finished a distance learning course in proofreading, scoring 'Merit'. She has contacted publishers and other businesses in her local area and is excited that this could be her first commission. Details from the client–freelancer phone conversation are:

	Enq. date: 1 August 2023	Enq. no: 1
Client/company name:	Academic Journal Publishing Co	
Contact name:	Judith Butcher	
Source:	CV sent to company	
Project title:	International Journal for Psychologists	
Description:	Academic journal	
	15 articles for proofreading (usual proofreader is ill)	
	Client says their standard payment is: £2.50 per page	
Length:	232 pages	
Artwork/tables:	A few small diagrams; a few tables	
Work IN as:	PDFs	
Work OUT as:	PDFs marked up using BSI symbols	
Client to supply:	Style sheet	
Schedule:	In-house: Tues–Thurs next week	

Freelancer A thinks the fee sounds fine, but decides it is wise to check whether the proposed fee is better than the break-even rate in her business plan (£27 per hour). She therefore asks the client for a sample paper, reads a couple of pages and decides that she could work at a rate of ten pages per hour.

As the client has suggested the budget available, the cost calculation described above needs to be reversed:

Hourly rate = Final cost: (no. pages × page rate) ÷ time
= £580.00 ÷ 23 hrs
= £25.22 per hour

Freelancer A is keen to win the work and decides to take on the job at the client's suggested fee, even though it is about £40 below her break-even rate, and therefore sends the following email to the client:

> **To**: Judith Butcher, Academic Journal Publishing Company
>
> **Subject**: Proofreading psychology journal
>
> Dear Ms Butcher
>
> Thank you for your enquiry and for sending through the sample paper.
>
> I am keen to work with you on this journal because psychology is one of my main specialisms. The rate you are suggesting works out a little below my usual rate (currently £27 per hour for proofreading), but because this would be my first project for your company, I am willing to take this project at your suggested rate of £2.50 per page (total for project: £580.00).
>
> Please note my payment terms are 30 days, and I am not VAT registered.
>
> Your proposed schedule is fine for me. Please could you confirm that you would like me to go ahead, and also could you please send me your house style?
>
> Best wishes
>
> Freelancer A

Comments

- On the plus side, Freelancer A has decided to accept a rate that is lower than her break-even figure, but she has left the door open for negotiations in future.
- However, it is to be hoped that Freelancer A's proofreading rate speeds up as she becomes more familiar with the material, because she overlooked the fact that she estimated 23 hours of work, which is closer to four days' work than the three days the client is allocating.
- Also, Freelancer A did not take account of non-productive preparation time studying the client's house style.
- Freelancer A forgot to take account of travel time/expenses (the office is a 30-minute bus ride away).

Is the client's rate and schedule reasonable?

For obvious reasons it's highly likely that the client's usual proofreader works more quickly than Freelancer A. If they work at, say, 13 pages per hour, the task would take them around 18 hours (6 hours per day), which is more achievable and likely to result in a more accurate end product. Note that the total fee would be the same (£580), but the 'hourly rate' would be £580 ÷ 18 = £32.22 per hour.

Related scenarios

- *What if the work could be done remotely?* No need to include travel time or cost (if that had been included in the estimate).
- *What if the client had provided a word count instead of extent?* Recalculate the time required based on number of words; make an allowance for checking artwork/tables (which may not be part of the word count).
- *What if the enquiry was for copyediting?* Recalculate the time required based on copyediting speed; take account of the nature of the journal (for example, papers from authors who use English as an additional

Tips

- Before you take on a project for a new client, try to find out more about them (eg check their bona fides via their website, Companies House or a simple internet search). This will also give you an idea of their likely budget for the job.
- Always evaluate the project and think about the schedule proposed, and then do the maths to check whether the client's suggested pay rate is reasonable and that they are allowing enough time to get the work done (including adequate time for screen, comfort and meal breaks), before you accept it.
- If the client doesn't provide T&Cs, consider sending your own (see '**Terms and conditions**'), perhaps based on a model contract. In particular, draw their attention to your payment terms, because late payments can mean the difference between thriving and surviving for freelancers.

language may require more intervention) and don't forget to account for dealing with author queries.

Complex estimating – making sure everything counts

Freelancer B is an Advanced Professional Member of the CIEP and has worked as an editor (freelance and in-house) for more than ten years, often on complex illustrated books. He has worked for this client before. Details from the client–freelancer phone conversation are:

	Enq. date: 1 April 2023	Enq. no: 999
Client/company name:	Well-known international organisation	
Contact name:	Horace Hart (marketing department)	
Source:	CIEP Directory	
Project title:	An illustrated guide to our work	
Description:	Foreword by chief executive; chapters contributed by various departments of the organisation	
	Complex design; designer/typesetter needs to be briefed	
	Editor to liaise with chapter authors to agree text	
	Current MS is too long; client suggests omitting some photographs and illustrations, plus pruning text (eg minimise repetition across chapters); two chapters need to be rewritten	
	Editor will need to check references and verify any URLs	
	Apply client's house style (especially to ensure consistency between chapters by different authors)	
	Please provide cost estimate and suggest schedule	
Length:	30,000 words (needs to be cut by approx. 3,000 words)	
Artwork/tables:	Photographs, illustrations, tables (all copyright of client)	
Work IN as:	Word files (separate chapters)	
Work OUT as:	One Word file, styled for designer	
Client to supply:	Artwork downloadable from client's SharePoint site; general style guidelines; authors' contact details	
Schedule:	To be confirmed; to tie in with major launch event in five months' time	

In order to provide an estimate and schedule, Freelancer B drafts a detailed plan of work. Here are the key points:

Stage 1. Assessment of MS	Read/assess MS, including: • identify design elements (eg sign-posting/images needed) to brief designer • identify problem chapters/sections (including repetition, factual errors, etc) • produce short report/notes to discuss at client Zoom meeting
Stage 2. Meeting	Zoom call with client and designer
Stage 3. Development editing	Rewrite two chapters (5,000 words) for approval + developing author queries for other chapters
Stage 4. Queries	Liaison with authors [Contingency: additional rewriting, chasing]
Stage 5. Copyediting	Copyediting (plus further revisions based on authors' responses to queries) Renumbering illustrations Final pass for house style, English, etc, plus styling the file for the typesetter
Stage 6. Proofs	Liaising with typesetter; collating proofs from authors, proofreader, client

Freelancer B then uses the above plan and several different rates in order to arrive at a final estimate of project costs:

Rates:

Rate 1 (proofreading) £30/hr

Rate 2 (project management/substantive editing) £39/hr

Rate 3 (copyediting) £34/hr

Hours:

Stages 1 & 6   18 hrs @ rate 1

Stages 2, 3 & 4   27 hrs @ rate 2

Stage 5   15 hrs @ rate 3

Contingency:

Stage 4   x hrs @ rate 2

(additional meeting/further rewriting, if necessary)

Stage 5   y hrs @ rate 3

(additional time for copyediting if extra work identified at stage 4)

Here is an extract from the email Freelancer B sends to the client:

> The plan of work (attached) is based on our experience with Project Z in 2021. Given that experience, I would suggest the following schedule:
>
> Stage 1: 1 week
>
> Stages 2–4: 3 to 4 weeks (depending on availability of authors)
>
> Stage 5: 2 to 3 weeks
>
> Stage 6: 2 weeks
>
> Estimated total project costs: £2,100
>
> Contingency (in case of additional meeting, extra time at stages 4 and 5): 15% of estimated total.
>
> Expenses: none anticipated
>
> We may need to review the costs and schedule after stage 1. I note the ultimate delivery date for your event.
>
> Best wishes
>
> Freelancer B

Comments

- Freelancer B has experience of working on complex projects with this client, so has accounted for several variables/tasks, including tasks that were not mentioned by the client (for example collating proofs, renumbering illustrations).
- Freelancer B has identified that the project may be more/less complex than previous jobs and has therefore offered only a ballpark figure (estimate) at this stage.
- Freelancer B has assumed this project is like previous ones so has not taken account of the client's specific instruction regarding checking of references/URLs (which may be time-consuming and generate many author queries). Indeed, he should have asked for a sample, because the 'references' might be a clue that this project is considerably different from previous ones.
- Freelancer B forgot to mention that he has recently decided to become VAT registered under the voluntary registration scheme.

Additional considerations

Travel time

Although travelling to meetings is less likely in the 2020s, it can still be necessary and is time-consuming. Should the client pay for the hours? This is a judgement call/negotiation point: travelling by train means that working for this or other clients is just about do-able on the journey; travelling by car is non-productive time away from the office (and increases greenhouse gas emissions).

Fixed fees vs quoting rates

At this stage, a ballpark figure (estimate) may be sufficient to agree the contract. Many freelancers are happy to work for a fixed fee whether suggested by themselves or the client (see **chapter 7**). This means the freelancer may make a higher 'profit' on the project (by completing the work in fewer hours than expected) but there is a risk that an overrun or incorrect initial assessment may erode the contract value, possibly to the extent that the final 'hourly rate' achieved barely covers the break-even point.

Leaving open a negotiation window can avoid this, but another judgement call is required: would you be willing to revise the total price down, rather than up, if necessary?

> **Tip**
> - For complex projects such as this, particularly where there is 'waiting time' while other people in the chain are preparing their contribution, away on holiday and so on, it is wise to suggest a schedule based on turnaround times for each stage, rather than a specific number of hours, to avoid the risk of the project manager converting your estimated hours to 'days' (overlooking the fact that you might be working on another project in parallel) – which may leave you gasping for breath to meet an overly tight schedule.

Estimating for non-standard projects – multimedia/websites

Freelancer C is a Professional Member of the CIEP who originally trained as an editor but decided to branch out into website design, editing and management, and she has completed several relevant training courses. She has been busy networking via social media to try to build up a client base for these new skills. Details from the client–freelancer exchange of emails are:

	Enq. date: 2 June 2023	**Enq. no:** 1902
Client/company name:	International Widgets R Us	
Contact name:	Will Collins	
Source:	Twitter	
Project title:	Proofread new corporate website	
Description:	Two large companies have merged and are rebranding. As part of this, a design company has created a new website, which will port across existing content from the two old sites. The new website has been built using a proprietary content management system (CMS). The design company is nearing the end of its contract and has submitted a price for the proofreading, but the client is seeking alternative suppliers. Originally, the company's publicity department wanted individual department managers to review/rewrite their content but, as the website launch date approaches, few have delivered new content.	
Length:	10 main sections; numerous subsections/pages (up to 200 pages in total)	
Artwork/tables:	In situ	
Work IN as:	Pages in CMS	
Work OUT as:	Input changes to client's CMS	
Client to supply:	Access to development site; secure login for CMS; phone number for web design company; contact details for department heads	
Schedule:	Launch at corporate event in less than 2 weeks	

Freelancer C spends a little time looking at the web design company's website, particularly at its client list, to get a feel for the likely amount International Widgets R Us may have paid for the development of its new website. She also takes a look at the new site (still under development) to assess the amount of text that needs to be proofread.

Here is Freelancer C's email to the client:

> **To**: Will Collins, International Widgets R Us
>
> **Subject**: New website proofreading
>
> Dear Will
>
> Thank you for your enquiry and for access to the development version of your new website.
>
> The web design company has done a great job; I really like the new design. As you mentioned, there are quite a lot of problems with the text, which really do need to be resolved before the site goes live. For example, several important pages contain information that is out of date, a few pages could definitely benefit from a rewrite, while others have grammatical and formatting errors. In addition, I noticed that alt tags and copyright/credits are missing from images, which leads me to suspect that metadata for pages needs to be checked, to ensure that your site meets current standards for accessibility and search engine optimisation (SEO).
>
> Given your impending launch date, I suggest that, rather than trying to proofread the entire site, we concentrate on the main navigation and top-level pages first, and then on two or three key departments (you to suggest which). While I am working through these, I will draw up a list of priorities for changes that can wait until after your launch date.
>
> My daily rate for preparing the essential content in time for your launch is £400, with six days' work needed in the first instance. This will include time needed to liaise with the web company and with department heads, to approve revisions, if necessary. Once the pressure of the launch has passed, we can discuss the further work, and that will be at the discounted rate of £45 per hour.
>
> Please note: to help meet your launch deadline, I am happy to work evenings and on Saturday, if necessary, for which there will be no additional charge. My payment terms are 30 days, and I am not VAT registered.

> Please could you confirm that you would like me to go ahead, and then perhaps we can agree a time to meet via Zoom so that we can talk through the key sections to target.
>
> Best wishes
> Freelancer C

Comments
- Freelancer C has correctly realised that this is not a simple 'proofreading' job and that the client needs assistance from an editor who has a general understanding of SEO and other website development issues.
- Freelancer C has assessed the likely competitors for this package of work, but she has also taken account of the urgent nature of the project and offered a tempting discount (which is still a very good rate compared with conventional book editing) for further work to try to help win the contract.
- Freelancer C could have more clearly identified potential problems with the text (by providing specific examples) in order to emphasise the need for a more detailed approach.
- Freelancer C was able to view the development site but has not yet had access to the CMS, which may not be as intuitive to use as other well-known systems.

Setting the right rate
An inexperienced editor might have simply put forward a standard hourly rate for proofreading, but that might have undermined the client's confidence in the freelancer's abilities, given the significant investment the company has already made in getting the site up and running.

Working practices
The client may decide that they need to know what changes the freelancer is proposing, so a different workflow may be necessary (for example, extracting text from the CMS and then developing it in Word using tracked changes/comments).

House style

This is every bit as important with website work as with books or other printed matter. Imposing or adopting a house style makes editing work more efficient and provides a more polished, professional end product.

> **Tip**
> - Avoid pricing work on websites and other multimedia projects based on simple page or word counts. There are numerous hidden elements, links to be checked/inserted and navigation to be tested that can add considerably to the workload (see 'Complex estimating').

Estimating for project managers – points to note

Project management is a special skill, and it generally attracts a higher rate of pay. There are several respected courses on project management for the publishing industry, not least the CIEP's own course, as well as many for more general businesses; likewise specialist project management software.

Estimating project management costs is not unlike complex estimating (discussed above), but with additional stages before and after copyediting (eg finding/briefing designers, illustrators, picture researchers, an indexer).

The 'known unknown' of quoting for project management work is the amount of time the project manager will need to spend on liaising with all the various parties, especially if problems arise. Although proofreaders and copyeditors may be happy to roll up the cost of a few phone calls or printing out material into their overheads, project managers need to pay attention to these business costs, simply because they make up a significant proportion of their role.

Various strategies are available (percentage fees or day/hourly rates), but a detailed exploration of these is beyond the scope of this guide.

Tips
- Be aware that project management means different things to different organisations. For some clients, it may mean taking responsibility for pushing the project through to publication – finding suitable freelancers for each stage and keeping everyone informed of progress. For others, it is synonymous with sub-contracting the publication process all at once, and in such instances project managers may even be required to take on financial responsibilities such as paying all sub-contractors, and bearing the cost if the project makes a loss.
- The risk of spending more time than planned on clients' meetings has increased considerably in the 2020s, now that it's quick and easy to 'hop on a Teams/Zoom meeting'. It is crucial to ensure that the client is aware that each such call will incur a time-based cost, as will responding to team group-chat (for example WhatsApp) messages, participating in top-level client meetings when working for an intermediary company, and sifting through lengthy email chains to find the one sentence that is relevant to what you need to do next.

Participating in competitive tenders

Fundamentally, there is little difference between submitting a quote or estimate and taking part in a competitive tender. Both approaches require multiple service providers – in competition with each other – to assess the client's requirements and submit a price for a project or series of projects. The competitive tender approach, however, tends to be used in two specific circumstances: (a) for projects with a larger budget (some companies have a requirement to tender all projects over a certain value) and (b) for public sector and charitable organisations, or for international organisations that are bound by national or international agreements requiring them to open opportunities to a wide range of possible suppliers through strictly controlled tendering processes.

Other differences are that clients often provide a detailed specification for the work and require tenderers to provide more detailed information in their responses – perhaps including proof of qualifications, references from other clients, business finance information and so on.

Tender documents are often drawn up in the expectation that large companies will be bidding, so responding to 'invitations to tender' can be daunting to freelance service providers. Don't be put off by the paperwork. The key to successful tendering is to remember the lesson taught in school: always read the questions carefully. Tenders may be rejected immediately if the tenderer has failed to submit some of the requested information or has not followed the approved format.

Be prepared to provide a health-and-safety policy or evidence of professional indemnity insurance. Equally, do not shy away from asking questions while you are preparing your response to a tender, if the client has the facility to answer them. Bear in mind, though, that corporate purchasing departments may be dealing with all sorts of tenders and may not have specialist knowledge about publishing processes.

A subgenre of the tendering process is where clients decide to draw up a list of 'approved suppliers'. Be aware that the process for getting onto such a list may be time-consuming (involving submitting a tender, attending an interview, sitting a test) and you may not be guaranteed work; frustratingly, you may also have to submit a detailed quote for every little project you are offered. On the plus side, being an approved supplier can open up a regular stream of interesting work, and payments may be both regular and relatively risk-free.

If you do decide to apply to be on a list, bear in mind that the list's shelf-life may be one, three or five years: and set your rates accordingly!

7 | What happens next?

Having carefully prepared your estimate or quotation and sent it to the client, you need to allow them a little time to absorb the details and arrive at a decision. But do not wait too long, unless you have already found out that the decision-making may be a drawn-out process (see '**Understanding the client's requirements**') – perhaps because the client needs to seek approval from a superior or is about to go away to a conference.

If you have not heard from the client within a couple of working days, by all means contact them to find out whether a decision has been taken. If it is not in your favour, do not be afraid to ask why you didn't secure the job. All information is of value to you – whether the decision was cost-based, due to your lack of/extensive experience, or whether you had misunderstood the client's requirements or budget.

Remember the 'Model enquiry form' (**Figure 1**)? You could add a couple of extra fields at the bottom of your form as a place to record feedback from the project you did not secure. Look through the feedback notes when you do an annual review of your rates and fees (see '**Valuing your skills and knowledge**'); and don't forget to check this burgeoning marketing database when the client calls three years later to ask you to quote on a different project.

But what if the client comes back to you with 'We think you have the right skills, but can you move a little on the price?' or words to that effect? Time for a little negotiation!

Negotiation basics

The key point to the negotiation is *don't panic*: the client is interested in you, but the ball is in your court and you need to keep your cool to avoid a drop shot. To extend the sporting metaphor – bat it back to them!

Ask what the client was hoping to pay, or find out whether they need a quicker turnaround than you had envisaged.

Negotiation is a complex art, worthy of a whole guide to itself. Contrary to popular perception it is not about haggling or desperately undercutting the competition – you are offering a professional service, not selling bananas on a market stall. The following thoughts from two respected authors may be of some assistance.

The first two are extracts from *Brilliant Freelancer*, by Leif Kendall, which is written for all sorts of freelancers, not just people in the publishing sector.

> [G]ood deals are equal exchanges that benefit both parties, and being secretive about budgets is pointless.

Brilliant Freelancer, 2011, p45

Kendall goes on to cite an example where the client has a budget of £500 but doesn't explain this to the various freelancers approached, who then quote more than double this amount – wasting everyone's time. He gives the following very sensible advice:

> If your client is reticent [to divulge their budget] ... offer them a ballpark cost.

Brilliant Freelancer, 2011, p45

Now compare those thoughts with guidance from Barbara Horn in her book, which is aimed at project managers in the publishing industry:

> When you have outlined the nature of the work, ... discuss the fee. Do not ask what the freelancer charges – that gives the freelancer control of the negotiation. Offer a fee. Start with an amount somewhat lower than the maximum available to allow room for bargaining, and keep a small amount in reserve for contingencies.

Editorial Project Management, 2006, p63

If that seems a little harsh, consider Sarah Lustig's more recent viewpoint on engaging freelance editorial professionals:

> Well-paid freelancers are happy freelancers. If you have always paid them a fair rate, when a problem does arise they will look for ways to help you fix it. If they have felt consistently underpaid and undervalued, you risk your freelancer dropping out altogether.

Sticking to a project budget – to save or splurge? 2020

Whichever side has made the opening 'bid', it is crucial to keep talking, to find out whether the client has room to manoeuvre on price or deadline or other aspects of the proposed project, as suggested in the case studies in **chapter 6**. Most important of all – especially for new freelancers – remember that the client needs to be confident in your ability to do the job to a professional standard, so do not start by offering a discount.

The same principles apply if, for whatever reason, you need to renegotiate any part of the project once it is under way (for example if there are unavoidable delays or the project turns out to be more complex than envisaged).

Terms and conditions (T&Cs)

Corporate clients may ask you to sign various documents relating to T&Cs, ranging from confidentiality clauses and indemnity clauses to equal-opportunities monitoring forms and health-and-safety documents.

Do not worry when a raft of legal papers drops into your email inbox; many clients have standard documents that are applied to all sorts of suppliers. Treat these as you would any other legally binding document: do not sign anything you are not happy with. If necessary, seek legal advice (for example through the CIEP's legal helpline service, if you are eligible for this benefit).

If the client does not send any T&Cs, you may wish to send your own. This could be as simple as stating your payment terms in your email to the client (see the case studies in **chapter 6**). For clients who are not used to commissioning editorial services, it can be helpful to clarify many aspects of the project – from who owns copyright to the work, to how many sets of changes you are willing to do, to delivery times. Again, this could be a simple email or letter, but it could be a formal contract document.

And finally …

Clients are undoubtedly cost-conscious, but they are fully aware of the need to pay a sensible amount for a job well done.

Have confidence in your own abilities; talk to colleagues and learn from their experiences; and always be professional in your dealings with both clients and colleagues.

Bon voyage!

8 | Resources

Useful business tools

Timing devices for PCs/Macs include, for instance, Toggl (**toggl.com/track**) or OfficeTime (**officetime.net/dev**). However, the list of productivity apps seems to grow daily, so keep an eye on freelance forums for new ones that might fit your circumstances/budget.

CIEP Going Solo Toolkit: information about how business income and expenditure are treated for tax in the UK, along with some practical tools for keeping business records: **ciep.uk/members/going-solo-toolkit**.

The Editor's Affairs (TEA): a series of Excel spreadsheets designed specifically for editors to keep track of their business data: **whatimeantosay.com/tea**.

CIEP contracts and T&Cs between freelancers and their clients: includes guidance on contracts, standard T&Cs and information about professional indemnity insurance (currently under review): **ciep.uk/members/contracts**.

You can also use the NUJ and Creators' Copyright Coalition 'Confirmation of Commission' form: **londonfreelance.org/forms/cccform.html**.

CIEP Environmental Policy and guidance for running an environmentally friendly editing business: **ciep.uk/standards/environmental-values**.

Minimum income and minimum wage

Find out how much you need to earn to survive using the Centre for Research in Social Policy tool: **minimumincome.org.uk**.

National Minimum Wage and National Living Wage rates: **gov.uk/national-minimum-wage-rates**.

Minimum Income Standard (Joseph Rowntree Foundation), 2017: **jrf.org.uk/report/minimum-income-standard-uk-2017**.

Minimum Income Standard (Joseph Rowntree Foundation), 2022: **jrf.org.uk/report/minimum-income-standard-uk-2022**.

Becoming VAT registered under the voluntary registration scheme: **gov.uk/how-vat-works/vat-schemes**.

Rate and salary comparisons

Andrew Bibby's Freelance Ready Reckoner, with the NUJ (2020): **andrewbibby.com/reckoner.html**.

Salaries in the publishing industry is a survey of more than 1,000 workers in the publishing industry carried out in 2021 and updated in 2023. The headline figures are free to view on the website: **bookcareers.com/salary-survey**.

CIEP suggested rates (members area: log-in required): **ciep.uk/resources/suggested-minimum-rates**.

NUJ Freelance Fees Guide: 'Advice – General/What freelances need to charge and why' (particularly the section titled Print media: Editing/producing books at **londonfreelance.org/feesguide**).

Editorial Freelancers Association (EFA): rates in United States dollars: **the-efa.org/rates**.

Institute of Professional Editors Limited (IPEd): rates in Australian dollars **iped-editors.org/about-editing/editors-pay-rates**.

Books

Cather, Karin and Margulis, Dick (2018). *The Paper It's Written On: Defining your relationship with an editing client*. CreateSpace Independent Publishing Platform (ISBN 978 1 726073 29 5).

Horn, Barbara (2006). *Editorial Project Management: With exercises and model answers*. London: Horn Editorial Books (ISBN 978 0 955340 40 6; out of print).

Kendall, Lief (2011). *Brilliant Freelancer: Discover the power of your own success*. Harlow: Pearson Education (ISBN 978 0 273744 63 4).

Blog posts and online articles

The good reasons why editorial work is time-consuming: 'Quick, quick, slow: the science of reading': **melaniethompson.co.uk/quick-quick-slow**.

For a quick overview of AI as it relates to editorial work, see a CIEP blog post from June 2023: **blog.ciep.uk/definite-articles-ai**.

Productivity rates: a handy summary of approximate times needed to achieve certain editorial tasks, with links to other useful resources on the same theme. **scieditor.ca/2011/07/productivity-rates-in-editing**.

Billing by the hour or agreeing a fixed price? Two articles that weigh up the options: **americaneditor.wordpress.com/2013/04/01/the-business-of-editing-the-ethics-of-billing** and **lifehacker.com/5994064/the-complete-guide-to-setting-and-negotiating-freelance-rates**.

'A project manager's view: Sticking to a project budget – to save or splurge?' is one of a pair of articles on how editorial project managers work with freelancers: **sarahlustigeditor.co.uk/post/a-project-budget-to-save-or-splurge**.

The marketing aspect of pricing: **thefreelancery.com/pricing-kill-the-zeros**.

Don't discount! A highly recommended article: **thefreelancery.com/no-more-self-inflicted-discounts**.

Value versus price: why the cheapest probably isn't the best: **aptwords.co.uk/value-versus-price**.

Increasing editing income – raising fees and declining lower-paid work: **louiseharnbyproofreader.com/blog/increasing-editing-income-raising-fees-and-declining-lower-paid-work**.

About the author

Melanie Thompson has worked in publishing, journalism and PR since 1988, for employers and clients ranging from government departments and professional bodies to publishers, charities and the business-to-business press. She became freelance in April 2000, and is an active Advanced Professional Member of the CIEP. As a freelance writer and editor, she focuses on climate change, energy efficiency and construction-related topics, and enjoys working on a wide range of materials, from technical guidance books to corporate websites. She also teaches proofreading and copyediting skills.

melaniethompson.co.uk

Acknowledgements

Thank you to all the many CIEP members whose questions and answers via the CIEP forums (and previously SfEPLine) have helped me to develop my professional skills since I became freelance in 2000 – particularly for their support and encouragement in implementing professional pricing practices.

Thanks also to editorial colleagues Adrienne Montgomerie for their useful insight into the situation for editors in Canada and the US, and Sara Jayne Donaldson for her assistance with earlier editions.

I am very grateful to former colleagues Nancy Duin and Louise Bolotin (both sadly deceased) who eloquently and entertainingly shared their pricing and negotiating skills with CIEP (SfEP) and NUJ members (including me) at training events, conferences and via private correspondence for more than 20 years.

www.ingramcontent.com/pod-product-compliance
Lightning Source LLC
Chambersburg PA
CBHW052107110526
44591CB00013B/2393